Walking the Mist

WALKING THE MIST

poems

Marjorie Stelmach

 THE ASHLAND POETRY PRESS

Printed in the United States of America
ISBN: 978-0-912592-87-9
Library of Congress Card Catalogue Number: 2020938308

Cover art: Alfred Böschl
Cover design: Nicholas Fedorshak

Acknowledgments

Acknowledgment and thanks to the editors of the following publications in which the poems listed below, some with slightly different titles or in slightly different form, first appeared:

The American Literary Review	"The Long-Term Taking" & "Keeping"
The Briar Cliff Review	"Canticle of Thirst"
Chariton Review	"Why I Can't Sing"
Cumberland River Review	"Home for the Holidays" & "Lullaby for Two Voices"
The Gettysburg Review	"Of Octopuses and Introverts," "Metaphysics," & "Oregon"
Image	"Art and the Covenant"
Innisfree	"Kindness" & "Eclogue for Summer's End"
Kenyon Review Online	"Interior Shot"
The Louisville Review	"Mica from the Graveyard"
Notre Dame Review	"The Field of What Could Be" & "Oh, Stay"
One	"Alchemical Winds" & "The Station Clock"
The Poet's Billow	"And a Heart Two Thousand Years Forewarned," "The Burren," "Not Far from Lisdoonvarna," "Death and the Three-Legged Goat," "Skellig Michael: Walking the Mist," "Incarnadine," & "Sunday on the Rocks"
Prairie Schooner	"The Psalm at the End of the Mind"
Rock & Sling	"Lines for the Spider"
Salamander	*"Highlights for Children"*
SALT	"Holdfast"
Sisyphus	"How Long?" & "My Mother's Sparrow Song"
Sou'wester	"One Chair, One Evening"
The Sow's Ear Poetry Review	"Trails You've Walked"

The sequence "Sunday on the Rocks" was awarded the 2017 Pangaea Prize from *The Poet's Billow*.

"Lullaby for Two Voices" was reprinted in *Cumberland River Review: The First Five Years*, ed. Graham Hillard, 2019.

*In memory of John and Dorothy Herweg
and, always, for Dan*

Contents

Walking the Mist

Mica from the Graveyard

Brittle slates
of chipped light
lifted
by my trowel
     to glint—

engraved in
in-
decipherable
script
     —a scripture

writ on isinglass,
each
flashing sheet,
a pane
     so thin—

you'd think
the silicate cells of it
would shatter,
but instead
     —they shine.

Alchemical Winds

And as for the mother who rocks a dead child in her arms—
We all rock a dead child in our arms.

—Fernando Pessoa

Alchemical Winds

A water that does not wet the hands.
—Michael Sendivogius
17th-century alchemist

"Whence this wind?" bark the crows in Latin—
　　twelve hooded crows with slate hairpieces

convened on the sheltered side of a rock discoursing
　　in dead tongues, priggishly mincing sideways

and back like clerics awkward in lay company. "Whence
　　this wind?" they repeat. And well they might:

it's a fearsome wind, storm wind, though it isn't raining.
　　Still, wrapped as they are in their black oilskins, perhaps

they aren't certain. Perhaps they think they've found it at last—
　　the famed alchemical *water that does not wet the hands.*

Now the world will be theirs without toil or trial.

Of a sudden, they make up their one mind and rise—
　　a dozen crazy old men taking off full speed

straight into the wind, and for long moments
　　it hardly matters, the fact that they're moving

slow-motion, backwards, their classical eloquence
　　stunned in their throats.

Twelve black nails driven back to the rocks.

After observing a string of these routs, the muscles
　　of her shoulders ache. In this way, she learns

she's been wringing her hands. Such an intractable world!
      If she had been born to these shores, she'd have known it

from earliest youth: how draining need is when it lasts
      and lasts, how intertwined are the forces, how urgently

for the whole of a lifetime, one hand washes the other.

And a Heart Two Thousand Years Forewarned

What father among you, if his son asks for bread,
would give him a stone?
　　　　　　—Luke 11:11

Some days Doolin's treacherous coast disguises itself
as flesh-colored foam. Other days rain slicks the rock

to an unmarked slate or fog slides in like the ghost
of a glacier, and she knows to walk here is unwise.

But on summer mornings, the limestone boulders
sulk in the sun like kneaded bread dough left to rise

from a metaphor sown two thousand years ago.
Chipped stones lift from their bone-yard, shift

into alignment, link and hinge, take on the guise
of the human. It's a risk on such mornings even to witness.

Crossing this faithless landscape, her memories break
along fault lines of trespass: rooms barred at thresholds,

names unspoken, occasions when splinters of error skitter
like spit on the hot flat skillet of her incomprehension.

Year after year, someone lay dying in a quiet room
adjacent to her childhood, someone essential who now

will never love her. Ask of the past what you wish, the answer
will be riddled with gaps—losses as lasting as hunger.

Bread?　　Stone.
And a heart forewarned.

The Burren

Walking the rubble-strewn coast this morning,
her eyes light first on a sorrowing Madonna,

next on a curled fetus, then on a hooded nun:
a theme emerging?

If he were with her here, he'd summon up
aqueducts, bridges, the cobbled roads of empire,

but for her, stones break like bread to meet
her hunger for the human.

And no, he is not here. She has come alone
to stroll these Irish graveyards, climb

steep trails to shrines, ride ferries to the wild
outposts of faith—to be sad for a time

she has promised will not be forever.
She knows it's futile, this christening

of stones, this wish to keep a private watch
over the absence assigned her—nameless

like so much else in this landscape.
What made her think so barren a coast

might ease her grief? Another fault line
of human vision, this belief that a life

can be ours to lead. Compared to these ancient,
enduring creatures, in what way are *we* the living?

Not Far from Lisdoonvarna

Not far from Lisdoonvarna—
famed wedding market where farmers' daughters
        were yearly brokered, yoked to the moonscape fields
of their fathers—not far, are the Green Holes of Doolin
        where ferries dock for daily runs to the Aran Islands.
Above the docking, on lacework stone, goats negotiate
        faults and fissures, alert to the crippling slip.
In wind-lapse, she hears the tide below her sucking
        and licking the tunnels, and she feels her peril—
she's strolling the salt-eaten slopes of a mountain.
        Of a sudden, her bones are numbered.

The Green Holes of Doolin,
her guidebook claims, is a sunken honeycomb carved
        from immense limestone slabs abandoned
when the last ice age ended and the first lichens
        flattened themselves to the sun.
For a million years, from salt-eaten caves, the sea
        went on calling for blood before blood
had yet learned to pulse. Even now, at the cliff base
        the tide comes in brutal enough to stun mackerel.
This is a sea too hard for the fish, a land too hard
        for the plowing.

In Lisdoonvarna,
it's long understood that hard-faced women come
        to the bargaining lashed to the stoniest holdings,
and always they prove entirely steadfast: an ugly law.
        Which is why she believes it completely.
As she believed the old man in the pub last night,
        who called her a beauty and, kneeling in sawdust,
recited ballads from a memory seemingly flawless,
        seemingly endless, until the barmaid led him away.

He was weeping. There's little negotiable here—
        each item of daily living a given: faith, history,
another Bailey's, eventual marriage, enduring beauty.

                Especially beauty.
Lichens have split and flowered the limestone
        with cadmium, zinc, and amber lanterns—
a light older than eyes, a beauty predating *beauty*.
        Who'd have guessed that over the eons
air would soften, and caustic gases would bend
        to a form living beings could accept
in a bargain struck for an *ad hoc* future. Struck
        and still holding. Witness this three-legged dog
that comes to the whistle of a woman whose land
        they've agreed to go on calling a farm
for as long as it's theirs to call.

                In Lisdoonvarna,
lacking a farm, a wily father, words to the ballads,
        she knows she has nothing to barter with.
Or to bargain for. Only her own heart's
        stubborn hold on a shore she agreed
to call home and her faith in a man she knows
        to be steadfast. For him, she'll tread
carefully here, where time is measured in eons,
        peril and beauty go hand in hand
to the bargaining block, and no one would think
        in a million years to hide their weeping.

Death and the Three-legged Goat: A Play in a Single Act

Stage Set: An abraded shore two thousand years old

where a brief withdrawal of ice and its sudden return
re-froze the sea in sink holes and fissures and stunned

the scant grasses to a dense black cap that appears soft
and ashy, ready to crumble. The eyes are such fools.

To the touch, this stuff's unyielding, welded to the plain
like a black hair-shirt four inches thick that will not come off.

Scores of fossils emboss the boulders: lives impasto'd
on stone with a palette knife of sudden death.

She tongues it, swallows:
Sudden. Death.

Enter, on the cliff above: a three-legged goat.

Fifty feet up the cliff face, he pauses. Their gazes meet.
He bleats. She bleats back. They face each other armed

with clamor—*maaaa* and *mehhh*, wind-music, sea-whistle,
each engaged in a solitary pan-dance, risking breakage

on a broken shore shot through with whistle-slots and worm-holes.
He on shaggy shanks and hooves, she on her slim anklebones,

while beneath—fifty meters? fifty miles?—the Atlantic
rushes and riddles the world's cold feet. She wonders,

can the goat even recall his crippling, his narrow escape?
She remembers a break of her own: an anklebone's snap and

her gasp at the shock of so sudden a misunderstanding between
her flesh and the earth, then the stab of her every step

on the long hobble home. How long did it last for this goat—
a hole, a misstep, a rock-manacled leg, a desperate testing

of the earth's grip, the gathering urgencies: hunger, night,
a rising tide, and most, most, the screaming piece of his own flesh

tethering him to stone? Fear must have swiftly won out:
one immense, wresting twist. Could *she* have performed such an act?

Never. After her first futile screams, she'd have cast her mind
forward, rehearsing the steps of escape: the shred and blood

of tissues—torn sinews, crushed bone—the dragging crawl
homeward, the gruesome healing, a long and diminished lifetime.

She would be spooling horrific calculations over and over
as night fell and the tide rose.

No. She is sure. No.
Exit: the three-legged goat, unnoticed.

ৡ

Back on the stony edge of the real world:

The goat, in his disgraceful coat of hanging shag
with its patches of orange and dirty-white,

has grown bored with their dance. Climbed higher?
Moved off? She has missed his departure.

In her time here, she's noticed a number
of three-legged dogs on the roads or dancing the edges

of herds—working dogs. Maimed creatures, well-matched:
the three-legged dog, the three-legged goat.

Can there be, between them, even the dimmest of recognitions?
Unlikely. She shakes her head, it's a hard, hard world.

She, too, should turn back, stepping carefully over
these treacherous rocks before shadows fall

to tangle and complicate the light. But she waits
and tongues it one more time—*hard life, sudden death,*

and tries again to imagine herself as a woman equal
to such a world. She imagines herself, instead, in full dark.

Exit, pursued by the sea.

Skellig Michael: Walking the Mist

Mid-morning. She visits the coastal rocks
in the fine beginnings of rain.
                    From this same shore
in another age at the far Western edge
of the faith, a single abbot
          and a dozen monks
brought to this rock
what God they could carry
                    in a wooden boat.
Skellig Michael, her guidebook reads:
eighteen miles out
          in a hanging mist,
and, as the locals will tell you,
walking the water.

There's little evidence left now—
a faint smudge in the gray rain marking
                    a weathered ledge
where six beehive cells
stood seven hundred feet up the side
          of the Skellig.
Stood, tormented,
like the twisted flesh of the god
                    insisted into the world
by that first abbot
with a burning gaze and a vision
          seaworthy enough to steer
a dozen monks to this rock
for life.

Can it still be had, conviction enough
to last a lifetime?

A perilous lifetime,
short at best, lived five hundred years
after the fact—
        the one fact that mattered—
but a way of life that endured on that rock
for a thousand years more in isolation,
                hunger, cold.
And they called it Love.
But who, after all, *was* there to love?
        Only the one
perfect man on a cross and, somehow,
each other.

It must have been awful: a life spent
clinging to a wind-thrashed crag, as the earth
                grew colder, the thin crops failed,
and the fear of a Viking attack attended
a man's every climb—stooped, hooded,
        in a salt-stiffened robe—
to a lookout alongside a grave-ground.
How un-sustaining to a man of flesh,
                loving an absent savior,
while those who shared his vows grew older
and Christ grew younger
        and younger. How implausible
to wear at your belt a cross designed
for a god's broken flesh.

And yet, that god's silver flesh hangs now
at her throat as she stands
                on the cinder turn-off,
seagulls wheeling above her screaming
for bread tossed from buses,

her guidebook gripped
in a hand unmarked by the hardship
of oars, trying to see it as it was back then.
            Her own faith belongs
to another self, her only proof it ever existed
in the catch of longing
            she thought she'd traded
            years back for a lowercase love.
And yet, here she stands.

In the summer months, thirteen ships
make the run to Skellig Michael, but
                her guidebook cautions:
The steep crumbling trail can be slick.
You climb at your peril. On shore,
the wind has picked up,
real rain is upon them. She can't imagine
that peril, that courage. Her doubts
            have had years to harden,
and all she can find of her own truth now
is this: that today Skellig Michael
            is visibly walking
the mist. She'll go that far.
It doesn't seem enough.

Art and the Covenant

i. Mid-Morning

Inside the rented van, a stone-gray moth head-butts
the windshield, drops stunned in a looping catch, and rises

to the same task intent, not on light—there are other
windows, some of them open—but *this one light.*

Now it pauses in a midair hover, its hinged wings wide
and minutely scripted in a flowing hand like God's

first text composed under the older laws of gravity and death,
the new ones not yet raised overhead and flung

down the mountain to strike and rebound largely intact,
though fractured at the fault lines of a future breakage.

For another long moment she watches the moth batter
hard sky, impelled by forces built into its tiny

unreasoning mind where flight has fashioned itself
from unspeakable will and a faceted eye.

ii. Late Morning

The van stands open in a field. Outside, wild grasses
and her blue plastic chair; in the distance, low roofs, rising slopes.

Closer in, long waves of a bone-colored wind roll down
from the hills to worry the pastures.

17

To sketch these scrolling heights and vales would require the whole
of the human body: palm and thumb, the muscle of the tongue,

veins that run the inner thigh, the flanks' and shoulders' pliancy,
the weight of the heart's standing stone.

More: a grasp of history, its pillage and want, its humbling,
its stubborn hope. More still: a Hokusai's genius of fixity,

endless canvas, an eye for light, costly pigments, a season's rent,
far more wine than she has at hand in this paper cup, and years,

years of an artist's life.

iii. Mid-Afternoon

From her chair, she scans the surrounding grasses: everywhere,
a fur of floating seeds in search of soft ground. Nearby,

an assiduous snail hauls its bright coiled shell up a weed
by the left front tire, intent on a task that can only end

in gravity—the grace of a gradual arc of descent or the sudden
tumble of the umber shell onto a distillation of earth's

suspect dust, its layers of pollen and crushed body parts.
It's an older world here than at home.

Yesterday, driving the Wicklow hills, her host remarked
on the generations it took these tough, ambitious farmers

to learn they'd need to leave the stones untouched in the fields
if they wished to grow anything, ever. Above, in higher cuts,

squares of turf stood in the open, free for the taking,
such that a poor man, an artist, might gather them home,

might burn his way down to his pigments there
in his own hearth, warming the while his own bones.

Canvas, though, runs high. Come winter, he'll paint
his ashen faces on abandoned boards. Dark faces.

Already, they will have lasted the ages.

iv. Late Afternoon

Near the van's front tire, one vanished snail. She understands
it has passed the point that it never sees will always come.

Has it, assisted by gravity, arced to the blade of a neighboring weed?
Pitched unheeded to the composite soil? Or, urged somehow

to a middle way, retraced its path, backwards and blind,
to a balance-point allowing a pause, a brief erasure of error before . . .

But it's never over, and all she knows is her snail has vanished
into one of its three available futures.

Back in the blue chair sketching, she takes herself to task again
for faithlessness: an artist worthy of her art would find a way

to capture this absence.

v. Early Evening

Her host, last evening, explained the logic of the un-cleared fields:
boulders, it seems, gather heat to fend off an early frost.

But how does a young farmer clearing his land
for ease in the plowing come to that understanding?

How many generations of labor are wasted before
such knowledge comes down, unquestioned, father to son?

How many years of being wrong before, exhausted
by earth's inexplicable laws, he hurls his fate

down the hillside, turns, and lets the fields have their way.
How humbling, she thinks, to grow old

on so unyielding a farm, tending thin soil, watching until
sterner laws reveal the true task of stones:

to hold the sun in place.

vi. Nightfall

The sun goes down fast behind these hills. Driving back
to her bed-and-breakfast, disheartened by her day, her work,

she spots on the dash the remains of the same gray moth.
It must have battered its spent heart all day

against a dimming transparency with less and less ardor
as the hours passed. Its wings seem to her as unscripted now

in the growing dark as the lines of her own aging flesh,
whose task on earth is as hopeless to decipher

as the dust of God's lost tablets.

The Field of What Could Be

Halfway up the trail to another hilltop shrine
she pauses and turns again toward the sea—
flat gray, its stone coast pocked
with pools,
like a waffle sogged in butter
and left to congeal
on a breakfast plate old as the world.

Above her, a virgin *contemplates sorrow*—
it said in the guidebook. Or was it *peril*?
She hopes this landscape of rubble will prove
a prospect worth the exertion.
But Lord, it's a long hike, and the tall, spikey,
rock-colored flowers that border the trail
are glad to cut flesh.

Below, she makes out a clutch of thatched roofs
tucked into fields of what could be . . . cows?
She looks again. Sheep?
At last, a bit of stone wall to rest on.
And, yes, they're sheep.
Of course, they're sheep.
This is Ireland.

Their bleats are inaudible, swallowed up
as they slide down the scale of reduction toward
lesser, more featureless creatures—
homily lambs as bland as counters
on the steep road to sleep.
Irish sheep, wind-throttled, silenced.
Unmoving. Unmoved.

Or, wait, are they stones?
Stones. She sees it now. Obvious.
Homely as roadwork, strewn over a field
of what could be . . . anything. No fences here,
nothing tended. Her lush, industrious
Midwestern fields have not prepared her
for this sterile enterprise.

She looks away: hills in deepening shadow,
the sea, and beyond it, her life—featureless,
weathered as a wound
carved in the side of one more savior.
She shivers. She's only halfway there;
she'll need to hurry to reach the shrine
and return before dark.

Above her, a virgin thins in the wind.

Incarnadine

Macbeth, Act II, scene ii

Just offshore in shallow waters, she spots a flock
of ocean-licked boulders slick with the living,

and soon, in her salt-stiffened shoes, she's hobbling
over a cobble of tiny, shelled flesh, pocketing treasures.

What she learns: it's not just balance she lacks,
but fearlessness, focus.

Just now, a snail she imagined would make
a pretty trinket to slip in her pocket

turns out to be alive and so tightly stuck
to its rock she can't budge it

barring great hurt to them both. Soaked,
she stumbles ashore empty handed.

Back on dry land, she finds she's netted
more than she thought—

a Marco Polo load of loot: pollen blossoms
clogging her nails, ripe tresses of dulse,

mollusks like beads to stucco her shoes, skin
scraped from her palms where she caught herself

falling. Odors billow around her like skirts
dragged through eons of filth. She's cloaked

in the odious crime of creation—
that primal murder of meaninglessness.

It's all on her hands, on her knees, it will not
rinse off. And saltwater burns.

What she learns: to the sea's mute history
of ransack and damage, her hurts add nothing.

Worse: she has no one to tell it to, neither this sad
little lesson nor her sudden wish to go home.

Sunday on the Rocks

*Prayer and praxis are simply the inside and the outside
of the same thing.*
—Patrick Harpur, *Mercurius:*
The Marriage Of Heaven & Earth

Praxis:

A score of scavenging gulls, two score, more.
Diving, reeling.
        Hunger and pluck.
And half the time the weight's too much,
or they lift a morsel
and a high wave rises to snatch it back.
Sunday: no rest for the greedy.
It's afternoon down by Doolin Pier:
bottled water, horse race static, families
with sandwiches scattered
on the rocks.

A toddler squats
to reach toward a sea-pummeled boulder,
struck by what treasure?
        a frond of seaweed?
        a fossil shell?
        a twisted bit of rusted iron?
He leans for balance,
his slight weight pitched against the wind,
a fat bun untouched in his other hand.
But, oh, it's Sunday,
and this is the work: to glean.

Wind takes everyone's hair. An old man
peels his shirt and is terribly white.
        Lovers sprawl on outcroppings. Kites

carve elegant shapes above the pier
where the Inisheer ferry has docked—
engines idling as tourists uncoil
down the plank:
>French bikers,
>bird-watchers, the young
>with their backpacks.
Then, the whole enterprise
in reverse:
revving the engines, whistling for tourists,
coiling the ropes—and the ferry's off.

Prayer:

Wind,
lift our hearts.
>Wind turn us over.
>Wash us in shadow,
toss us in light.
Spin us into a briefness
of spirit.
>Return us
to flesh.

Let salt
be the white alchemical
>fire. Let wind
>be the water
that will not
wet the hands.
>Let sun

be gold—
as always it has been.

O, let it be Sunday.
Let us be lovers
        of our own lives,
        their personal hungers;
of our own brief spinning
into this world of
        of the wounded,
        the living, and out again
into what comes.

Lines for the Spider

We take nothing and add nothing; we pass and forget;
and the sun is on time every day.

—Fernando Pessoa

Lines for the Spider

On the far side of these mountains, rain is falling in my mother's city.
Standing in my doorway in spring sun, I let imagined rain-song fill me.

Just beyond the doorstep, spiders are at work in the tangled grasses
spinning sun-catchers, snagging bits of brightness, weaving

glimpse and *gone.*

Lingering jewels of dew nudge the light; they won't be long.
They tremble, as they should on a planet spun of time

where we hear not a sound from the spiders, though always
they are present. Earth's workings are immensely still.

Intricate and unrelenting.

I picture my mother on the far side of these mountains, arrayed in cerements
of rain. If I knew how, I'd cover her with fine, sun-woven silks,

but the distance between us is so much more than wishing, and I know
that already, even at this moment—

Listen: the rain song.   Listen: the spider.

Home for the Holidays

Back home, you take up November's posture, forearms tight
      at your waist, palms clamped to your elbows.
You drag out thick socks against the chill of morning floorboards,
      scavenge the closet shelves for scarves and gloves,
surprised to find what you need where you've always found it.

Down at the shore the walkers are older, slower, the greetings
      that pass between you a shade more formal.
Your unspoken wish for each couple you pass, for each
      lone stroller: that this be a holiday season without
undue change, without fresh sorrow.

Raw winds gust over the water in textures of etch and abrasion.
      Brisk winds, you insist, *bracing.* But you turn toward home.
"Spider cloth," Lawrence called skies like this—flocked and scoured
      like the decades-old wallpaper hung in the upstairs hallway
scrubbed of its pattern by a rush of children glad to be off.

Evenings, you walk the old neighborhood marking the changes:
      most of the climbing trees gone, the privacy hedges higher.
It's all low-maintenance siding now. Landscaping trucks in the drives.
      None of your school friends remain, and the church
is a different denomination.

You'll get through the holidays first, then arrange for the sale.
      You'll hold yourself tight, dress in layers, stay
close to home making certain each day they have all they could
      wish for. All this, for as long as your visit lasts:
this month, the next.

Lullaby for Two Voices

*I was born at a time when most young people had lost their belief in God
for much the same reason that their elders had kept theirs—without
knowing why.*
                                    —Fernando Pessoa

My earliest recurrent nightmare—hooves,
riding down on me hard in the dark—
turned out to be my heartbeat.

Above my bed, Jesus the shepherd
pastured his flock beside still waters,
but the dark in my bedroom was wet black ink,
and all winter the hooves drew nearer.

Years later, in a sermon I've otherwise forgotten,
a preacher explained the psalm's *still waters*:
sheep, he claimed, have an innate fear
of swiftly moving streams.

As if by this fact he might nail truth to faith.
Or faith to the fearful workings of the earth.

My mother, deep in dementia now,
repeats the 23rd Psalm without a misstep.
I'm the one who winces as she nears
the valley of the shadow.

I want to think hers is a pure and fearless faith,
but there are days she grips my hand so hard
she shakes, and I've nothing to offer her—
nothing of truth, nothing of death.

Sometimes we sing old hymns together,
humming mostly, faking the words.

By their second spring, lambs are all but grown,
grazing high pastures beside a race of snow-melt,
or ranging the slopes where repeatedly
they strand themselves on perilous outcroppings.

There they stay, terrified, hunkered at the brink
bleating: *error unto death, error unto death.*

If I were their shepherd, they'd be taken
by the wolves. I'm terrible at rescue. The most
I'd have to offer them is cynical advice:

*Wiser by far than the paths of righteousness
are the promptings of fear.*

It's my own uneven history of vigilance
that wakes me after midnight reaching for words
to talk my heart down from the edge.
Heart, I say, *don't fret; there's nothing here to fear.*

But the hoof beats. And the plummet.
And the wolves.

Is lying to your heart what it means
to lose your faith?

Often, my mother misplaces her words, replacing them
with smiles of apology to break my heart.
To restore a kind of balance, I bring too many words
of my own to the Center.

On my worst nights, I picture her awake in the dark
frightened by the pounding of her heart.

In my good dreams, we're singing—a slender song,
a lullaby. *There, there*, I sing. Meaning: *here, I'm here.*
Where we need fear no evil.

Here's what I think I still believe:
when our words have disappeared, the workings
of the earth will grow kinder.

Oregon

i.

Joseph of Arimathea cocks
an eyebrow: *reborn*? *Really?*

Still he keeps on showing up
after dark at Jesus's door.

Afterward, Joseph, who has missed
the grim ending,

offers in atonement a tomb.
His own: it is finished.

ii.

Outside the tomb stories gather:
drunken guards, angels, headlong Peter,

John hobbled with love, Mary,
a gardener, and for centuries,

us—the rest of us, wearing
our motley of fable and faith.

We know, though weeping
and hobbled with love,

we will not be permitted
to miss the ending.

iii.

Our father rails
at the hospice pastor, insisting

that God has abandoned us all.
He shocks a visiting deaconess,

claiming, "It's not too late
to light out for Oregon—there

a man has a choice.
For his wife. For himself."

This, in a hissing whisper
between clenched teeth.

Appalled, the deaconess
grips his arm, desperate

to roll the stone back
down his throat, but our father

knows betrayal when he sees it
on the gardener's face:

"My God. My God."

iv.
Another spring. Our mother
in her transport chair waits quietly

at the day-room glass to watch
sparrows gather at the feeder;

she can barely see them.
"Oh, a cardinal!"

I hear her joy and remember: joy.
We chat for a bit,

and again, moments later:
"Oh, look, a cardinal!"

And a third time: "Oh, a tulip!"
But the bird is still a cardinal.

Will always be a cardinal.
Bright plastic, speared into dirt

beside a sign:
"God loves a garden."

v.
Easter week. Seasonal stories
gather in the dayroom.

We cock an eyebrow: rebirth,
resurrection?

No. Snow will fall
on the feeders this Easter.

Jesus will return. Our father
will turn his face away

toward Oregon, desperate
for the blessing owed him,

the miracle cure. Our mother
will pray with Deaconess Gayle

the indelible words
of the Lord's Prayer. Our father

in the months to come will move
past rage, past internet scams,

past recriminations. He'll show up
each dawn in her numbered room

to sit by her side watching over
her difficult breathing.

He knows: it is finished.

My Father Contemplates Loneliness

All the forms are fugitive, but the substances survive.
—Emerson

Robed in overcast, light-raked, or mottled with clouds
      these bluffs above the river score my morning sky;

all night, their presence threads my dreams,
      a gentle thrumming in my ears, counseling my heart

toward acquiescence. Is this what it comes to, the practice
      of a lifetime: the refinement of a single recognition?

ह

Nothing special marked that morning in Emerson's last year
      when, asking after Thoreau at breakfast, he faltered, paused,

then whispered, *What was the name of my best friend?*
      Overnight, a mountain had shifted.

ह

These days, I catch myself watching your eyes
      to learn if today will be one of the days I'm still here,

robed in whatever continuance you've found for me to wear.
      I believe in the garments of repetition, these rags we draw

from the costume box, every item festive once, now threadbare,
      even comical—more treasured as the gaps widen.

If I were to wind time back to where we had not yet foreseen
      this day's sorrow, could we live it over, you and I—

but this time together? A slow walk into the cancelling shadow,
    neither of us keeping the watch. But how much erasure erases *us?*

₫

Some nights, wakeful, I imagine God in a tattered robe, a drifter
    in interstellar dust, seeking a garden spot dimly remembered,

where two young people spoke his name with an open,
    uncomplicated love, prompting him to call out to them,

except . . . He can almost remember . . . They were,
    weren't they once, the best of friends?

₫

Millennia from now, when earth is again one continent wandering
    ocean wastes, I like to think these cliffs and slopes

will still be here, cutting their cursive into the sky. By then,
    will Emerson's transcendent God at his immense

and increasing distance, have suffered with Earth a reciprocal
    red-shift—our long, tangled history lost in a wash

of lengthening light waves? Or might he draw near on occasion,
    bound by promise or habit, to watch our familiar moon

perform its slow-motion blink? In the gradual passing
    of his eternity, might he have come to understand

what Adam meant by *lonely?*

My Mother's Sparrow Song [†]

What if the unsung were the only song?
—Alan Shapiro

Polly wheels her keyboard into the common room in Wild Horse Creek.
Today, it's *Seasonal Favorites* and *The Great American Songbook.*

She's come to lure bits of memory back, to draw, if she can, a self
from the cells of the past. After a lag, with luck, a few of the residents

seize on a scrap of tune that unearths for a moment, the old days.
I'll take you home again, Kathleen. Or *Someone to watch over me.*

It's hard not to smile at *Who knows where or when?*
But listen: my mother has begun to sing. She taps a finger

on the armrest of her wheelchair, but I can't turn to face her,
afraid that whatever past she's found will break like a wave

and disperse. Remember that one? she asks. *Remember,* a word
we're advised not to use in the Alzheimer's wing. What I remember,

I tell her, is how you would not allow *us* to sing at the table.
She laughs as the next song starts. This one she recognizes at once:

   The autumn birds drift past my window . . .

And, in this way, a song about leaves comes completely apart,
winging off and returning with birds. *Since you went away*

the days grow long, and soon I'll hear old winter's song . . .
How long her days must feel, so much lost of what she loved—

home and friends, travel, birding, and, this past winter, my father.
I close my eyes and weary birds drift down like feathers

42

to settle on the tiles. The only one I recognize is Bede's
simple sparrow completing a lifetime's pull through the mead hall

and out into the cold skies of memory's emptying songbook.

---

† In the story of Bede's sparrow (found in Venerable Bede's *Ecclesiastical History of the English People*—731 C.E.), the human condition is compared to the flight of a sparrow. Just as a sparrow entering from the stormy winter skies flies the length of a warm, lit mead hall and back again into the harshness of the night, "this life of man appears for a short space, but of what went before, or what is to follow, we are utterly ignorant."

Odysseus in Eldercare: A Monologue
after Tennyson

                    I'd planned
a generous stretch of years in which to
live like an idle king: morning papers,
lunch with the ROMEOs, evening strolls to
the Overlook. In short, a tranquil and
gradual aging. Instead, we're stranded
at the Bluffs with this sad cast of cast-offs.
A wretched fleet of wrecked vessels. Daily,
I wake to an inchoate rage that ebbs
to despondency by dusk: my daily
undoing.
                For you, it's a shadow life:
meals, activities, naps. Caregivers, hired
for next to nothing, paid to speak comfort
to the dying. Polly, at her keyboard-
on-wheels—thick songbooks, a thin soprano.
Visits from the fearsome Deaconess Gayle,
deluded woman, turnip-shaped and stuffed
with missionary zeal. To rile her I
praise the state of Oregon, where they let
a dying woman choose her time to die.
She's speechless.
                    No friends left from our past
and no one here knows us from Adam. I'm
the last of the ROMEOs now, and you
have wandered off the map into margins
where I can't follow. I'm grateful most days
you know me still, seem glad of me at dawn,
dozing in my chair in your private room.
I'm always there before you wake—dawn to
dusk, like a lighthouse in reverse. A man
keeps his promises, that's all. I've promised
not to die before you.

When his comrades
laid the sleeping Odysseus gently
at the base of Ithaca's cliffs, he was
young, but he must have known the best was all
behind him: after decades of war and
the ill will of gods, what's left for a man
to drag to the shores of home but the dregs
of a life? Once, we travelled the world. Now
it's the garden-room, the hair salon, you
in your transport chair and I, your feeble
pilot.
        Nights alone, I rage and sob and
argue my rectitude to the stars like
a daft old man. Ahead are the dark days
of winter. Ahead is the end. For you,
Heaven's a harbor; there you'll be met by
the God of your youth. For me, the one god
is science—and science has failed me. *But
look! A crescent moon!* You smile, but I know
you can't see it. The pathway home will be
dark tonight, each crack in the walk a risk,
and for your sake I mustn't fall.
                            Above,
tier on tier of rooms where the elderly
lie awake. When we moved to this complex,
we christened these bluffs *Mount Purgatory*—
our private joke. Now, no one's laughing. It's
hard enough not to cry. Our time has come
to yield to time. Still, if these years were our
purgatory, it could have been worse—we
were together. I promised forever.
Forever is over. Forgive me. One
last broken promise can hardly matter.

The Psalm at the End of the Mind:
A Broken Monologue
after Wallace Stevens

The psalm at the end of the mind
past last thought rises.
A foreign song.   *The Lord is my . . .*
        what is the Lord?

        Here in the care center—

mere decor.   Daily the sun rises
wrapt in bronze distance.   And me?
A ward   of this ward a-clatter with metals
        in nameless shades.

        Start over: *The Lord is . . .*

a bird in a mirror.   Mere bird.
I will lift up mine eyes unto . . .   Shelves
of photos. Faces. Nameless blanks.   I want
        to go home, Lord.

        I shall not want.

I will lift up mine eyes.   Tiers.
Blurred faces.   *How long, Lord,*
how long   this call
        and response?   *Ask*

        and ye shall receive.

Whose turn to speak, Lord?
Yours?
Yours.   You,
        from whence cometh

46

an ending.

Me? I will sing in the branches of the Lord.
In the *mansions* of the Lord.   In the *wings*
of the mansions.   A bird
        in a mirror,

        fire-forged, flying

into distances of ...   *Hills*.
Help cometh from hills,   from
halls.
        Wheels rolling golden

        down long halls

toward sunset   bringing the honey
of lotus that will let me
at the edge of space   end
        this psalm.   This *amen*.

        This   self.

How Long?

*At the end of this day there remains what remained yesterday
and what will remain tomorrow: the insatiable, unquantifiable
longing to be both the same and other.*
　　　　　　　—Fernando Pessoa

Storms tore down a city's worth of leaves last night,
and now I'm up to my shins in a litter of green corpses,

a hundred thousand of them, more, ripped untimely
from their branches, still vivid

with the wasted stuff of photosynthesis, still primed
to drink the sun.

How long before they know in their cells it's over?

I've read that lab rats dropped in cylinders of water
will tread only briefly, then simply give it up, go under.

But feed those rats on yogurt, they'll paddle to exhaustion,
their resignation overruled by resident bacteria

refusing to jump ship: a legion of stubborn otherness.

Three years I've lived entangled in the vying mandates
of this world. My mother says she's ready now to go.

Am I wrong, then, if my heart insists
not yet, not yet—

These days, hospice counsels us to hold a loved one's
lifeless hand until the last cell cools. Hearing this, I hurt

for past abandonments, hands released too soon to the ministry
of creatures whose own directive is to break flesh back

to its elements—none of which was ever love.

The world feels alien this morning, the shine of the living
piled lifeless at my feet like suppliants:

I have not lived well in the presence of my dead.
Today, it seems an insufficiency of love to hold a hand

for anything less than forever.

But once, there was another measure—
six pomegranate seeds, after which no quantity of love

could make the slightest difference: it was a simpler age.
Three times I've gone on with it—my life.

And now again. I'll hold my mother's hand knowing
too much, too little. My life, like hers,

an otherness. However long.

The Long-Term Taking

How long, O Lord? How long?
                    —Psalm 13

This morning on the shoulder of the two-lane, a downy
lay flattened in gravel and dust, like a wildflower pressed

in an old book. If it's true birds take in a visual field
flat-out, in total focus, this one's last vision

was likely the grille of a lumber truck—a steel beast
lugging a horizontal forest.

Tonight, the wild creatures of the Northwoods will feast
on fresh woodpecker flesh.

By week's end I'll walk past that stained patch of dirt
without thought, so swift the erasure.

Out on the lake, the twilight stirs with the loons'
famous laughter.

≈

I've taken to browsing my grandfather's shelves—
ledgers kept a century back, a child's illustrated Bible,

a Boy Scout Handbook from 1911 with chapter titles
from another age: *Chivalry and Brave Deeds*; *Endurance*.

Under the title *Losing One's Way*, I find this:

> *If lost in the woods for a time one can survive*
> *by chewing the leather of one's own shoes.*

It's only long after, when I've climbed to the loft,
that I find myself mulling the missing comma:

If *lost* for a time? Or *survive* for a time?
And my own darker question: For how long a time?

I wake after midnight to a stillness frayed
by occasional tremolos filled with longing.

     Or bone-deep misgivings.
     Or simple lust.

I've no way of knowing, but if you've heard those liquid echoes
warbling the dark, you know it's not laughter.

ə✿

I've read if you change a single ion—magnesium to iron—
you'll have changed chlorophyll to blood.

Had Jesus come upon this bit of chemistry,
might he have chosen to come to earth, not *incarnate,*

but *in-arborate*—embodied in leafage, root, and limb?
How to know anything, least of all what will save us.

ə✿

Out in the dark on the highway's edge, the feast continues,
the downy's remains consumed by a host

of microscopic creatures burrowed deep in its tissues
and by the beaks and canine teeth of the North:

a ceremony washed by Northern Lights
spilling their ions onto earth—an ablution to ease

the long-term taking.

ﻉ♥

How long now since the loon's last call? As I lie in the loft,
wakeful, expectant, the lake's stillness stretches.

Maybe there's time.
Maybe from one of my grandfather's volumes

I still might learn the skills of discernment—
how to distinguish between the silence that precedes a call

and one that follows it forever.

One Chair, One Evening

The truly wise man would enjoy the whole spectacle of the world from his armchair; he wouldn't need to talk to anyone or to know how to read, just how to make use of his five senses and a soul innocent of sadness.

—Fernando Pessoa

One Chair, One Evening

Inside this room: one desk, one bed, one deep red coffee mug on the sill.
Outside the door: one white plastic chair piled all night with darkness,
piled at dawn with brittle leaf-fall. Nothing much changes.

It's a used world, handled to smudge and buffed back to barely presentable.
All the old props—sun, moon, rain. I do with them what I always do: blink at,
pine beneath, stand out in. I use them neglectfully. Still, they return.

I return, too, unlocking the door, raising the shades to spill the sky's
blank gaze on the floor. Inside, time's grains await me, heaped
as if for a gradual leveling with the dull side of a knife.

By mid-afternoon, I've wasted my words on a thistle-world rattled
by cold, on a crow's raucous caw, the dregs of a bitter coffee.
It's endless, this work: the praise of the unremarkable.

Look at these hands. How can it be that fingerprints stay unchanged
despite decades of damage and healing? Now they claim—the security pros—
that each human retina, too, is unique and will last out our lives.

But I think my eyes are different here, scoured by late autumn dawns,
raw noons, a snarl of hedges, weathered fences, untended lawns.
My eyes *must* be different here, or why have I come?

Like the patient saints of repetition, I ask, not a glimpse
of God's face, but the heart-slam of being caught in his sights.
Being seen, recognized. This is my prayer:

that my dubious life might be ratified, God's seal impressed
on my moltenness. Followed—I fear, I expect—by annealing cold.
Slowly, I've come to accept that only his distance

allows the pilgrimage. So it is I come back to this room,
with my singular hands, with my eyes. We came here together once,
you and I. I've saved you this chair that was yours, and now

is merely a surface outside my door that I clear of debris
each morning before starting over. One unremarkable chair
where the world will go on piling its layers of leaves

and darkness long after my time here is over. Meanwhile, alone
in this room or another, I'll wait for the stroke of the slow knife:
a woman unique, I'm assured, beyond damage and healing,

trying to praise what brings me to evening.

Kindness

1.

A woman turns a page of her novel and stares at nothing
for a long while, as you do when a story is over.

Her book will lie closed on the bedside table when
later that same afternoon they find her.

Her daughter and son will live on in that town
with a father who keeps her secret—a kindness.

From him, they will learn to say they have "lost"
their mother. Their father, too, will be lost to them,

his face brushed with sadness. And so they'll grow older
with no one to ask.

They will wait twenty years to ask each other.

2.

Across the street, in habitual silence, a boy is practicing drums.
His father has not come down, though it's nearly noon.

The boy scores cadences in his head. He's perfecting the art
of halting the sticks just above the drum skin.

He loves the brushes most of all, how they feel to his wrists—
those soft figure eights, loves how lightly the sticks rest

in his fingers and on the heels of his palms as he strikes
the taut cushion of air just barely above the surface.

He feels himself gaining a mastery, knows when he parts
the curtain of silence he'll stop their hearts.

He is learning kindness.

3.
A century turns.

On the outskirts of town in the eldercare center,
a woman brushes her thin gray hair.

She has inched her wheel chair closer all morning
to the light in the east. It's arduous work.

By the time she reaches the window, the sun has climbed too high
to spread on her shoulders that warmth she remembers.

She brushes and brushes. By ten, her hair is shining and ready
to braid on the porch in the sunshine, but where is her mother?

By four, she begins to whisper, "Help me," over and over
until someone hears and steers her to dinner, where someone

removes the brush from her lap—but always it's back
on her bedside table when the sun comes

over the sill to wake her.

4.
Down the hall, a woman leans hard on the wheels
of her transport chair, steering it toward the closed door

of a sunroom, but no one is able to help her just now.
As she waits, she recalls a slant of light she loved as a child,

a cushion of straw under her feet and the smell
of horses. Someone's large hands have lifted a saddle

up and away, have draped a blanket on a wooden divider,
are taking a curry brush down from a wall-hook.

It's good to push hard with both hands, to feel
larger hands covering hers, guiding her strokes.

She shivers in pleasure at the way flesh ripples
low on the horse's flanks: this is *her* horse, hers only.

This horse loves her.

5.
In a storefront church on a downtown street, the boy
who mastered the half-inch halt sits in a wooden folding chair

on the stage where he plays his drums each Sunday.
Whether he's brushing the underside of the choir's

tight harmony of petitions or scourging a flat-out strut
for an Easter procession, he finds himself smiling.

He's survived a few close brushes with faith and knows
he will come again and again in this life within range

of God's love, never quite touching—a kindness.

6.

The brother and sister still live in that town where they long ago
learned their father's secret. Together, they keep it.

The boy, nearing old age himself, works in an eldercare center,
tending its systems, mending what's broken, attending

to minor needs: gently he straightens their pillows, returns
lost belongings, adjusts the blinds. Some of the residents tell him

they're ready to leave now. He listens in silence. Sometimes
he nods. He spends his breaks in a numbered room down the hall

where he reads to his sister. Some days she knows him.

Highlights for Children

i. May I sew you to a sheet . . . ?

Saturdays in the waiting room:
shelves of tiny chipped dishes, trucks,
Little Golden Books, stacks
of tattered *Highlights*.

What's Wrong with This Picture?
was easy: shadows on the wrong side
of a bush, a goldfish swimming the slope
of a cloud, square wheels on a wheelchair.

The *Hidden Objects* page proved harder:
a pipe in a curtain's fold,
a comb camouflaged in basket-thatch,
an umbrella in the fireplace.

And those silly rhymes:
Marden me, Padam, is this pie occupued?
Yes, may I sew you to a sheet
in the chack of the birch?

I hated *Goofus and Gallant* most:
perfect Gallant smiling, sharing,
never interrupting; Goofus
late, untidy, rude.

Lately, though, I was striving
to be *gallant*—a word I'd never seen
before those Saturdays
when Judy disappeared with Dad

through swinging doors and returned
two hours later with clean, new platelets
in her blood, holding two lollipops:
we were sisters; sisters shared.

Dad would steer her wheelchair
from elevator to parking lot,
both of them silent for so long
I thought they'd never speak to me again.

Like Gallant, I never failed to thank her
for the lollypop, or—since it was all I had—
to recite for her the "Marden me, Padam"
on the long drive home:

My, this is a chutiful birch.
Yes, many thinkle peep so.

ii. My this is a chutiful birch.

In the easement below my window this morning,
two deer stand near in a tangle of bushes,
invisible until an ear or tail flicks white,

while overhead a trio of crows crosses
a pale sky that cuts them out as crisp
as burnt crow-cookies.

It's one of the iron laws of childhood:
never draw attention to yourself.
Stay quiet. Hold perfectly still. Disappear.

How many years, before I understood
those Saturdays, that closing door, the quality
of their silence—understood it was Dad

who supplied the lollipops, the platelets, too.
Once you've seen a hidden truth it's always there—
apparent as a zebra caged among the winter trees.

iii. What's wrong with this picture?

Picture a Saturday afternoon, not long before
the end. Sodden litter blows across the hospital lot,
sudden gusts whip our faces, as Dad
positions her wheelchair closer
to the station wagon door, where it's my job
to hold a huge umbrella over us—
Judy in his arms now, crying a little still,
and the wind to deal with—
all of us soaked.

The Station Clock

Back then,
before boarding a train alone,

children were asked
to state, unassisted, their name,

address, and destination;
to name the adult

who would meet them; to read
the hands of the station clock.

Not a word to the stationmaster
of her cancer, the surgery scheduled;

it was not the practice, back then,
to offer a reason.

Back home again, it was spring
and school still in session—

spilt sugar that morning,
left un-swept on the breakfast table.

The previous night, while they slept,
their mother had died.

Their mother
had died,

and sugar sparkled
on the breakfast table.

(I stood there. I watched it
glisten.)

No one, back then,
thought children should know.

It would be unkind:
they would be afraid.

Better, back then, to be sent off alone
on a train.

(It was spring: I had only just learned
to tell time.)

Interior Shot

Our memories are encumbered with facts.
Beyond recollections . . . we should like to relive
our suppressed impressions and the dreams that made us.
—Gaston Bachelard

Five blades unmoving above a bed—
wrought-iron bedstead, the linens
broken open. The shadow
             of a wardrobe
cast across a folded spread.
Heavy glass windows hoisted on ropes,
their frames fixed
        at oblique angles.

The blades must have been turning slowly
when the shutter fell and the flash caught
those ghost-oars in the act
           of parting
the heavy sleeping-porch air,
stirring a haze of half-lit dust—
a dust, settled now
          more than half my life.

Three small children slept there that night,
their skin cooled in the August swelter
by a darkness rotating smoothly above them.
              No one is pictured
in this snapshot, though. Nor do I remember
my dreams that night, whether they woke me.
Nor what I heard: the burr
        of a long-awaited rain?
the whisper of tires pulling off down the drive?
Nor whether my eyelids lifted to headlights

crossing the ceiling, baring
                these blades
in a slash of light, before the fan
(that never, of course, stopped turning)
resumed its circle and drone
                of denial.

And now, this room whose existence
had thinned over time to doubt, worn down
to dream, returns to my hand—
                indisputable proof
of whatever it was occurred that night.
Or never occurred. Or would,
while we slept, go on
                forever occurring.

Why I Can't Sing

From the cluster of houses uphill from mine, flares erupt:
    a high window blazes a square of white phosphorus;

copper flashing on a chimney pot glows. It's only
    the dusk, only the sun shifting its grip, slipping off.

Mine's an average heart, seventy beats a minute;
    a songbird's in flight might approach a thousand.

If I can't fly, it's not alone for lack of wings. I haven't
    the heart for it. Much less, these recent years, for song.

Everyone's leaving.

Tonight, it's beach fires I recall, sparks falling up
    red-gold into darkness, disappearing above a lit ring

of family features we never doubted would outlast our lives.
    Those nights, each plucked string of your guitar

slashed a silver tracer from across the embers,
    and even now by an unlit hearth, knees hugged tight

to my slow, pedestrian heart, I can taste that marshmallow
    sweetness, its sugars sealed in a crust I burnt on purpose.

I feel it still, the crisp shell collapsing as my teeth
    broke the surface, a burst of syrup singeing my tongue—

which must be the reason, tonight, I can't sing.

Absentee

October—
even the word is scruffy, riddled with holes
and thinning on its verticals—a scaffolding
where anything might hang: scarecrows,
a pair of thieves, our family crest
(sickle moon with crows).
 It's noon.
I'm sitting in the lobby of my local bank,
absentee ballot in my lap, lulled
by the whisper of numbers changing hands.
Hard rain splatters the plate glass
at my back.
 Once, in this downpour,
I'd have heard the burr of Mother Earth
hushing her children's fears: *there, there.*
Not this year. Too many graves.
Only duty brings me here. Polls
have already picked the winners.
 I've blackened
the ballot's ovals as instructed, shiny lozenges
like bullets. Their names will sour before full term
when back in the grade school gym
I'll tap new choices onto a screen.
Taps: November's anthem.
 At last, duly notarized,
I pull from the lot into the hiss of wet city streets.
In my heart, I hear grief's stages ticking down.
Holes in the fabric wherever I look. Worse,
God help me, the holidays ahead.
Thanksgiving.
 Longest Night.

Trails You've Walked

You cross the public lot over broken glass
and sunlit puddles ruffled by wind. High overhead

hawks ride the thermals, and midway the leaves,
half-green, half-turned, spin down around you.

You watch them. Half-watch. You know the ending:
just before touchdown they'll lift back and ride

the prairie winds one final time before the inevitable
settling. *Taken back,* we say. *Taken home.*

The gates to the nature preserve stand wide,
and you stride off, mown grass replaced

by a cushion of woodchips. You know your way
on these trails as you do among family graves.

Besides, there are markers.
Of course, you're not lost. Not really.

But if you are, it's approaching noon: the sun won't
help you. Still, you'll be fine; just wait it out.

Around you, prairie grasses spread
their singular, persistent quiets, filled with sway

and shifting light like cerements in golds and umbers.
In bronze, flax, stone. In bone and ash. You stop

and breathe the coming cold. Soon, you move on,
pausing only when the stalks are tall enough to hide you.

Each breath reminds you of the flat unlikelihood
of living. Which is why you've come.

As you follow the river's curve, you feel them,
your lost ones. With you again. Lifted back.

You try to partake of their quiet. You ask them to wait,
you won't be long, but you only half-hear their answer.

You'll need to come back. Listen harder.

Canticle of Thirst

A clear glass of water on the sill holding only
the light of this small room.

How to understand so perfect an alignment
of translucence and containment?

How to seek in one life both solitude and love?

Later, for the last time, I'll walk the prairie trails—
tall grasses, flocks of dark birds lifting.

Out there, the long damps are only just beginning—
Earth keeps so quiet about cold.

About everything ahead.

From my rocker, I gaze out over a lawn
pleated with dawn light, stippled with dead leaves.

Soon my sound-track will shift to the hum of tires—
my life and its score at cross-purposes again.

What I'll leave behind me in this emptied room:
the waning arc of rocker blades, a stain of old thirsts

in a drained water glass; beyond the locked window,
inaudible winds bowing the grasses, leaves

acquiescing, finding the earth.

Keeping

Because the one who loves never knows what he loves
Neither does he know why he loves, or what loving is . . .
— Fernando Pessoa
from *The Keeper of Sheep*

Keeping

But I remain sad like a sunset
As our imagining shows it,
When a chill falls at the side of the valley
And you feel night has come in
Like a butterfly through a window.
                              —Fernando Pessoa

Of birds, I can't claim to know much,
but today when a small bird drops from inside
the sky to snag on a tree's burred trunk,
how can my eye not follow
its bright, abrupt arc, not clamp
on that soft clot of heartbeat and feather?
I will it to *hold* for the seal of language, that I
might catch up with its plummet,
skid to its halt, and say:
                    nuthatch, birch.
It's the only way I know in this world:
after the fact. Lurching. Lunging. Wielding
my net of belatedness. Yes,
like the Keeper of Sheep, I aspire
simply to watch what passes. Instead,
I seize on what pauses, caress
what abides my caresses,
work on the wording. There's so little time,
everything passing. I, too,
am passing.
                    This is the sadness.
It's why I listen for bells descending from
higher slopes: someone, I think,
must be keeping
a watch on the long progression
of the dead. My own
come to me across time as if

it were nothing, glistening like tears.
They come across space like butterfly wings
brushing the tips of the grasses.
But I must keep faith with the living, too,
who are also the dying.
                    So far, I'm a terrible keeper
of sheep. My lambs wander serenely off
toward the bluffs, dropping over the edge
of my shameful unknowing
and into the sudden sky
where they'll catch and cling as they can
to whatever will hold
as they wait out my always
belated coming—
a roughened patch of vertical trunk,
or an outcrop of rock just below the cliff edge.
There's purchase enough in this world,
I believe this. The problem is time.
                    Do you hear it, too?
Across the world a butterfly's wing
has just stilled
after shattering everything.

Holdfast

But my sadness is calm . . .
And is what there should be in the soul
When it is thinking it exists
And the hands are picking flowers without noticing which.
　　　　　　　　　—Fernando Pessoa

Words are like sheep. They bleat incessantly,
lag and bolt, lose their way. Some days

I'm tempted to quit. Most days, I keep at it.
Today at my desk, though, I'm staring off,

watching leaves break from the honey locusts
to scatter over the grasses and mulling

the artful mechanics of autumn:
abscission cells massed at the holdfast point,

nudging a leaf bit by bit from the stem,
until all that's left to the leaf is thirst—

and the fall.
Holdfast: named for its failure to hold.

How many bits of the world have we named
for the ways they will fail us?

Still lifes. Utopias. Frost flowers. Mortals.

Lately, I'm drawn to the wordless. Like now:
I'm counting my heartbeats.

Or rather, I'm listening hard for the instant
when one beat is over and the next must rise

out of nothing, clenched to go on.
I count on my heartbeats—though they too

are named for the way they will fail me.
Tonight is the equinox.

Out in my yard, either it's summer or summer
is over. What would it mean to catch Earth

between beats? To feel, for an instant,
that terrible doubt?

I suspect my final heartbeat will find me
here at my desk about to give up.

Or else I'll be thinking about my soul—
how it just might exist—letting my words

pass almost unnoticed as my hand records them,
trying to say what I mean:

I mean to be faithful.

Metaphysics

To think is uncomfortable like walking in the rain
When the wind is rising and it looks like raining more.
. . .
There is ample metaphysics in not thinking at all.
　　　　　　　　　　　　—Fernando Pessoa

My heart announces she's given up
　　　　caring about the future. These days,
she's all about the past, claims ignorance
　　　　is bliss. Not so long ago, I tell her,
scholars thought the heart was a fire
　　　　burning blood. She's unimpressed:
another item in the list of ways we got it wrong.

We get it wrong about each other
　　　　all the time, Heart and I. Most often,
by evening we've reconciled. Tonight,
　　　　I read to her from Ptolemy's
"nostalgia theory of gravity,"
　　　　all earthly things aspiring to
the virtue of the sphere, the circle's purity.

This resonates with her. Best not to mention
　　　　an article I read the other day
concerning skulls: our cranium's been
　　　　rounding now for 1500 years.
Something, I guess, in the DNA
　　　　constructing helmets for our journey
into space when Earth's a barren ruin—

scrawny humans floating out
　　　　to pollinate the stars. Or is God
having second thoughts, reworking
　　　　old motifs? Halos were a pretty

piece of thinking. As were crystal spheres.
        Myself, I'm fond of skull-shaped skulls,
the poignant way mine seeks each night

its customary socket in my pillow,
        letting the one on my desk take up
the watch: *memento mori*. No need,
        I think, to change the *status quo*.
Heart seems especially quiet tonight;
        she's like that when she's sad.
Or has she drifted off? Tonight's rain

soothes me, makes me think of Leonardo's
        lifelong love of currents—rains
and streams and waterways: his
        was an elegant mind. He wrote
that water in all its forms yearned
        to round the globe, caress earth's
broken edges toward a perfect sphere.

Soon, Heart will have her way with me.
        I'll sink into her rocking tides
and dream I'm wandering the past,
        wearing the softened robes
of love, regret, or simple gratitude—
        childhood's clothes—and like a child
I'll wake in tears. Monks used to pray

for *the gift of tears*—a more practical
        prayer than it seems, if it turns out
humanity's secret task is to round
        the imperfect globe of the eye.
But prayer has never been my gift.

Instead, I feel a non-specific longing
for alignment with a purpose longer

than my life, something to be faithful to
        when everything else is over. Once,
we discussed such things, my heart and I.
        But who am I fooling? I call it
my heart—that pulse of time I feel inside me;
        call it *mine*. But I know it's simply
passing through. I know it means to fail me.

Eclogue for Summer's End

The ancients invoked the Muses.
We invoke ourselves.
                        —Fernando Pessoa

Today, the sky
tips toward me a table draped
        in azure cloth and piled
        with still-life clouds as plump
and self-absorbed as summer's flocks
on the upland slopes.

Years back,
I'd lie under racing skies
        while around me a scatter of lambs
        leapt straight up
in their birth-skin, bleating
from newness alone—that astonishment.

But then,
what young heart is not undone
        by springtime's forces?
        You're cast ecstatic from the heights
or slammed to your knees by loss.
Or both. Both.

I remember
how waves of wanting tossed
        my body like a bottle
        in a riptide. This was before
the urgent message sealed inside me
got lost in the world's

ongoing—
the same ongoing that has stranded me here,
    grown old in late summer's
    great soaking stillness
watching a slope of sky that seems
to beckon. But I can't go.

I'm working still
on what it means, the weather
    of *this* life. Or what *I* mean
    having weathered it.
Or maybe only what I *meant*
to mean back then, that spring,
when I, myself, was the meaning.

Of Octopuses and Introverts

In a blink, they'll mottle or pock or take on sheen
as background demands: paisleys, plaids,
a pebble-colored curdle, or the grained precision
of fine sand.
Such swift and flawless camouflage:
they'll replicate the rock they've flattened against,
adopt the tiger stripes of a venomous sea snake,
or ruffle their flesh into leafy fronds to ripple in a current's drift.

Caught in the act, they'll gather themselves umbrella fashion,
then, faster than startle, they'll shoot out of sight.
Most baffling of all: they're colorblind—
but how did they learn their predators aren't?
Trial and error?
In labs, they'll routinely open jars,
hatch complex hunting schemes, unlock
our finest locks behind our backs. In the wild, they'll tear

a tentacle from a Portuguese man-of-war to wield
as a poisonous sword. Dissect their flesh, you'll find blue blood,
three hearts, no bones,
impressive memory—short term and long,
a huge and utterly alien brain: *distributed intelligence*,
three-fifths of their neurons stowed in their arms.
True, our own survival kit is constructed, like theirs,
from time and flesh and reliant on traits

our ancestors bought in increments,
paying such magnitudes of death, it's hard to believe
we were worth the price. But somehow
we stumbled on consciousness, on companionship,
even on love, while their DNA
has brought them to this: they live alone, they hide;

they brew a silky ink to blind any creature that blunders
too close to their hermit caves.

They can't even pass the mirror test:
if you paint a spot on an octopus face and set up a mirror,
you won't see a tentacle reaching in wonder to touch its *self*,
as you would with a human toddler.
It's hard to prove they can recognize
even another of their own kind—an aptitude needed
chiefly for sex. As for sex, the male just rips off an arm—
the one that holds the rows of sperm—

and hands it over to a waiting mate, who stores it in her mantle
and later, alone, smears it onto her newly laid eggs.
Does it make it less sad that an octopus couple
mates only once, at the very end?
That the male then enters senescence and dies?
That the female follows when her eggs have hatched,
leaving their young to fend for themselves:
live alone, learn to hide?

Live close; visit often: a formula extolled
as wiser than marriage. Maybe so, but it seems
too little to ask of a life. And theirs
is a mayfly life at best: three years, maybe four.
Does an octopus know in all three hearts—
as some say we'll know in our blood, in our bones—
when its *self* is over? Four hundred million years
of error and trial to fine-tune an octopus to match

its flesh to any piece of its world—but never
a glimmer of *self*: I find it hard to understand. Still,
it's this lush *otherness*

that moves me in evolution's long
efficient pull—all our desperate strategies
for so little edge. What use, for example,
this empathy of ours? "I'm so lonesome I could cry,"
Hank Williams sings, wielding a whippoorwill's

borrowed call and the whine of a midnight train, crooning
in a voice so forlorn that in the hollows of my only heart,
I can't tell his voice from my own.
But empathy for an octopus? Really?
Foolish, I confess. But give me an hour on YouTube immersed
in that solitary tank, and I start to see my life
as an episodic game of seeking and hiding,
my self as a stranger in a mirror—

my arms, too, expendable.

The Thirty-First Chamber

Those Old Testament patriarchs
whose lifespans neared a thousand years—
I'm thinking they were trees.

&

There's a poet I read about years back;
diagnosed with dementia,
   he wandered his rooms,
window to window, holding a pencil.
He'd pause, lift it, study it doubtfully,
then drift on.
  Who can say how he understood it,
this implement so shaped to his hand,
but he'd needed it once,
might want it again.

I like to think he was gripping,
as best he could, a tree.

&

I carry a notebook to jot down thoughts
and random facts. Like this one:
 99% of a tree is dead already.
But the living bits—leaves and root-tips,
the layer of cork beneath the bark—
these are enough,
spring after spring, to rouse
my winter-stilled heart.

How do you recognize a fact
that might one day save you?

ॐ

Shortly after my mother's death,
a neighbor whispered that if I missed her (if?),
            I had only to breathe.
It's statistically true: I'd be holding inside me
molecules of her final breath.
        Of *her* breath—and all the breaths
ever drawn since the first human birth.
By that calculation, each indrawn breath holds
exhalations of vanished mastodons,
            endangered snow leopards,
three trillion trees.

ॐ

The chambered nautilus moves in a lifetime
through thirty consecutive cells lugging
          a coil of outgrown homes
winding back to the four tiny rooms
it was born to.
        Once abandoned, each cell is sealed,
no going back—but surely the aging nautilus
feels a growing buoyancy
in its wake.

We, too, were born to four small chambers.
They do what they can to keep us afloat.

ॐ

I have memories of my mother, if only a few,
but I doubt they're real. Not if the cells

88

that carry memories
die like the rest after seven years.
How can she wander the rooms of my past,
among neurons too young to have ever known
                    her voice, her touch?
Or do memories live instead
in our synapses?

So many gaps in my knowledge.

ੳ

I'm losing my past as my family thins:
Alzheimer's, cancer, heart disease.
            One day, I'll find myself
composed of the cells I will die in—
my cerements.
        When I'm gone,
will my ghost-selves wander the rooms
of someone's past, window to window?
            And holding . . . what?
A pencil? A photo of nameless kin?
Someone's hand?

ੳ

What does a nautilus understand
of the ghosted chambers it drags
            through the waters?
One day it will enter its thirtieth chamber
and die there.
        But that's *my* knowledge.

A nautilus has no reason to doubt
there's a room beyond.

ᕒᕀ

Our lives are lengthening,
more of us reaching the hundred-year mark.
When the thought exhausts me,
        I watch the trees,
their living bits just beginning to turn.
Soon, they'll litter a soil softened
by autumn rains,
                where foraging deer
will leave tracks as they weave
through the understory, exposed
against snow.

I'll watch from my windows.

ᕒᕀ

My notebook claims:
A mere 10% of our cells are 'our own.'
Statistically speaking, we're all of us Other—
        mostly bacteria.
And this, too:
Bacteria don't have to die.
        "My" bacteria sifting forever
from host to host,
gripping whatever bits of my past
                might seem useful.

As if they were poets.

In the parable,
a newly cured blind man sees in his first
sighted moments the figures of men.
     Moving like trees.
Patriarchs, maybe,
gathered outside our thirtieth chamber
   to breathe in our last exhalations.
Three trillion strong, steadfast, waiting
in their long patience
to walk us home.

Oh, Stay

Oh, stay, thou art so fair.
                    —Goethe

What is it to praise? Be particles.
                    —Rumi

The sun casts a rectangle onto the grass
to the left of the feeder,

and now the sky, unasked, delivers
a vee of geese arrowing over the locusts.

I follow their passing until their wedge
is cloud-smudged away and that door closes.

Back in the yard, everything's altered,
the lawn darker, my sun-patch—

a parallelogram now—leaning,
collapsing toward disappearance:

I'm smack up against it, earth's vast roll.
It's my heart that trips, catching up.

> *O, my laggard, my life,*
> *slow learner,*
> *if you can, slow further*
> *while this strip of light*
> *slims*
> *to another*
> *thin blade*
> *in the grasses.*

᪥

Among particles, only photons refuse the drag
of gravity, riding an eternal stasis:

time, to a photon, means nothing.
When Rumi asks, "What is it to praise?"

I'd answer: *Be photons. Stay.*
This, in the hope that into that timelessness

meaning might steal. *Meaning* tucked into
a fold in the fabric, a space into which

a healer might sidle to shake her seed rattle,
or a lord of the mime come lugging

his knapsack of gold-dust.
Though, how would we know?

If a tree fell into eternity...
But who has time for conundrums?

Nothing pauses. Always, the altering world
grips us tight by the heart, proclaiming:

It was all for *this*, that wild beginning,
that break with stasis,

that first *Let there be*— Then, once begun,
everything, everything, vee'd out of sight,

time unrolling a spreading wake of lag
and loss, whose drag will reduce us all

to irreducible bits, from which
Rumi urges us to forge our small

Hallelujah.

Additional Thanks

I am grateful to Bavarian artist, Alfred Böschl, who generously provided his float glass sculpture for the cover of this book. Recipient of the prestigious *Verleihung des Bundesdienstkreuzes* for his contribution to German culture, Böschl is internationally known for his sculpture and works of sacred art.

I am deeply indebted to the Virginia Center for the Creative arts for fellowships that provided me a studio in beautiful surroundings, the comradeship of amazing artists, and uninterrupted time to concentrate on the creation of these poems. My thanks as well to Ragdale for the fellowship that allowed me to bring this book to completion.

I have been blessed over the years with the wise suggestions and reliable friendship of poets, Jane O. Wayne and Allison Funk. Their own masterful poetry has been an inspiration. Every poem in this book has also benefited immensely from the gimlet eye of Barbara Crooker, accomplished poet and dear friend.

Special thanks to Deborah Fleming and Paige Webb for their care and patience in bringing this book to completion under the challenging conditions of the coronavirus pandemic.

And Dan, thank you. Your loving support has been the gift of a lifetime.